MAC'S CHOICE

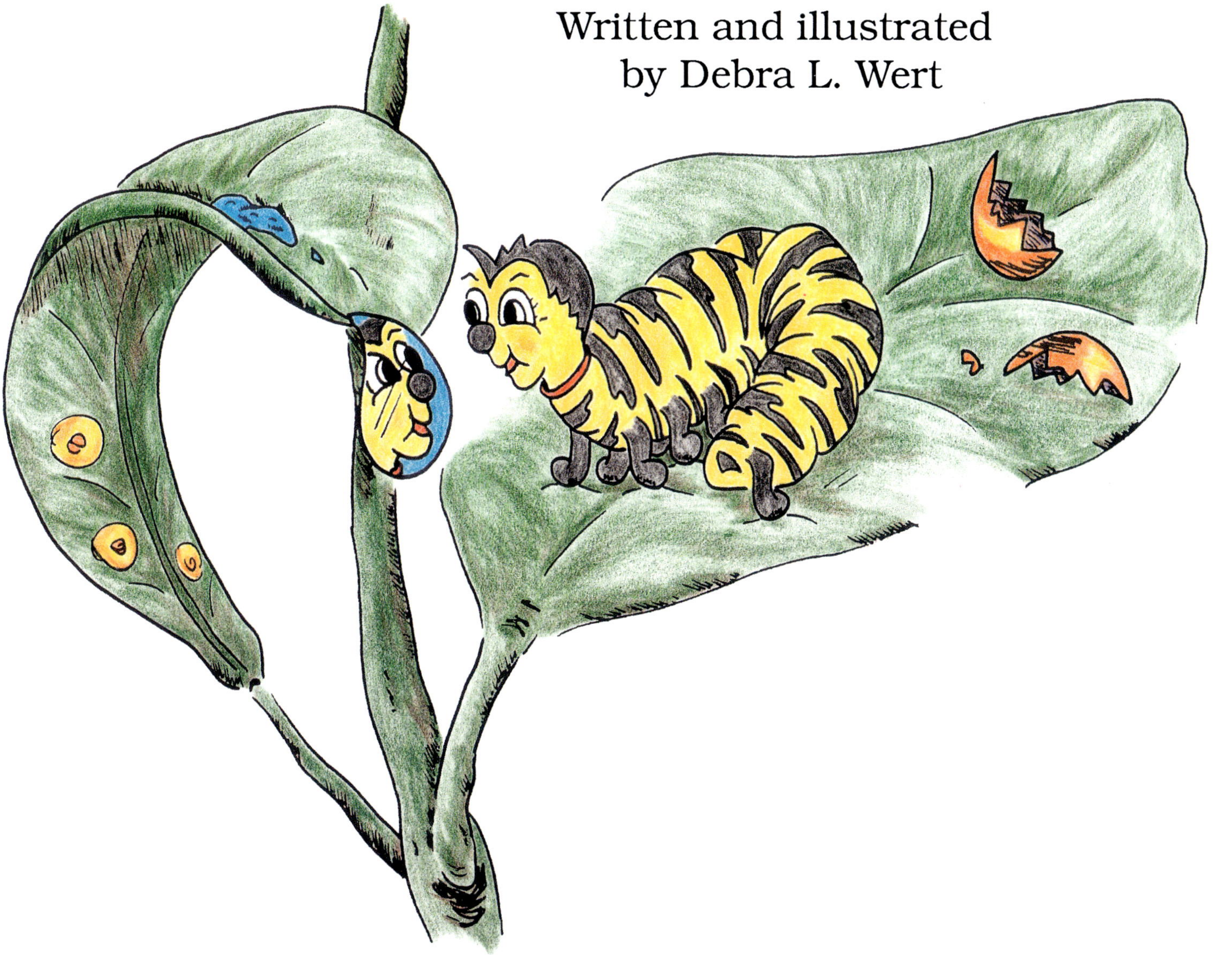

Written and illustrated
by Debra L. Wert

ROCKY RIVER PUBLISHERS
P. O. Box 1679
Shepherdstown, WV 25443
(304) 876-2711

To my family, especially Cindy, Jim, Becky, Pam, Jimmy, Danny, and Melissa and to my friends Jeannette and Kenny for their help and support. And for my parents, who have given me encouragement and a life filled with love. This book is also dedicated to the children of the world. May they be strong and choose a life free from drugs.

ISBN 0-944576-02-8
Library of Congress Catalog Card Number: 89-60200

Printing History
First Printing, March 1989
Second Printing, March 1990

Printed in the United States of America
By WINCHESTER PRINTERS, INC., Winchester, VA 22601
Separations by GRAPHTEC, 1724 Whitehead Road, Baltimore, MD 21207

IMPORTANT NOTE TO PARENTS AND TEACHERS:

This book is written for children between the ages of six and twelve, a time when most children have not yet experimented with drugs.

It has a sad ending, dealing with the reality that many lives are irreversibly affected by drug usage. **Because of the ending, we recommend that this book be read in a setting where a parent or teacher will be there to discuss the story with the child or children.**

When tested in the classroom, this book captured the children's interest quickly and stimulated thoughtful and meaningful dialogue between the children and their teachers regarding drug usage and its consequences.

Many methods are being tried to prevent drug experimentation. Our hope is that the shock value and the discussions ensuing from this story will make a lasting impression on the minds of children, and later, when these same children are forced to make a choice regarding drugs, they will remember **Mac's Choice** and say "No."

Best wishes to you, dear reader, and all those children whose lives you touch.

THE ROCKY RIVER FOLKS

One morning, very early in the spring, an orange-and-black monarch butterfly flew into a quiet, sunny meadow. Just a few hours earlier she had left her southern wintering roost to fly north. She would soon be followed by millions of monarch butterflies migrating to the northern states. But now it was time for this particular butterfly to lay her eggs. She flew all over the meadow looking and looking for the perfect spot. At last she saw a small milkweed patch. "That's the perfect place to lay my eggs," she decided.

One by one, the butterfly gently placed each egg under a leaf. Once all her eggs were safely tucked away, the butterfly flew off.

Inside the eggs the larvae grew bigger and bigger. After three days the larvae began to chew their way out of their shells. Mac, a big plump caterpillar, was the first to break free. Mac looked very handsome with his bright yellow-and-black striped coat. He scooted around his milkweed leaf admiring himself. Mac knew he was handsome.

The next caterpillar to come out of her egg was a female named Grace. She was beautiful. As Grace took her first look around, she saw Mac a few feet away eating his eggshell. She went over and introduced herself. "Hello there! My name is Grace. What's your name? Can we be friends?" she asked.

Mac smiled and with his mouth full, answered, "Mac's my name. Sure, we can be friends. You can never have too many friends."

"Great! We'll be good friends. I just know we will," Grace said as she began to eat her own eggshell. It was fun to share her first meal with her new friend, Mac.

It was late in the afternoon when the last monarch caterpillar finally chewed his way out of his eggshell. He was a small fellow, smaller than Mac. But his coat was the best coat of all the caterpillars in the meadow. His coat had brilliant yellow stripes, snow-white streaks, and black stripes as black as black could be.

When Grace saw the last caterpillar, she called down to him. "Hi there, slowpoke! We've been waiting for you all day. What's your name?"

The little caterpillar answered, "My name is Jeffery."

"Hello, Jeffery," Grace said. "I'm Grace, and that big guy over there eating everything in sight is Mac. Come on up here and help us eat these milkweed leaves," she invited.

Before long Mac, Grace, and Jeffery were the best of buddies. They ate and played and did everything together. The boy caterpillars' favorite game was Daredevil. Grace did not like that game very much. She thought it was dangerous. But the boys loved it.

To play Daredevil, Mac and Jeffery would hang upside down from a twig. When Grace shouted "Daredevil," they would let go and fall towards the ground. As they fell they bounced from leaf to leaf. That was the fun part! As they neared the ground, Grace would shout, "Ball up!" Then Mac and Jeffery would roll themselves up, bouncing like two striped balls when they hit the grass. This way they never got hurt.

One day while the caterpillars were lounging around eating milkweed leaves, Mac became bored. He decided to hunt for some different leaves to taste. So Mac left the milkweed patch in search of new food. He crawled around rocks and through tall grass. Before long Mac came to a net-covered field. "Hmm, what's this!" he said to himself. He saw a tall net blocking his way.

Wondering what to do next, Mac looked up and saw a sign hanging on the net. "STAY OUT: DANGEROUS," he read. Mac was confused. He didn't see anything in the field that looked dangerous to him. All he could see were rows and rows of plants. "What's so dangerous about a bunch of plants?" Mac asked out loud.

Nearby, in the shadow of some rocks crouched a palmetto bug. He had been watching and listening to Mac. "I should show this caterpillar what's in that field," he chuckled to himself. "This will be fun! I'm going to see how much trouble I can get him into!"

In a flash the palmetto bug jumped in front of Mac. "Hey, Bud," he called. "It's not dangerous in that field. Actually, it's a lot of fun! Come on; I'll show you what I mean."

Mac watched the palmetto bug wriggle through the net and then wave for him to follow. So Mac wriggled through the net, too.

"By the way, my name is Roach," the palmetto bug said. "What's your name?"

"My name's Mac, but my friends call me Big Guy," Mac answered cautiously. He was not sure he should be in this net-covered field. After all, the sign did say this place was dangerous. But Mac didn't want Roach to know he was scared, so he pretended that everything was cool.

Once inside the field, Roach and Mac crawled to the very top of a large plant. "Go ahead, Mac," Roach coaxed. "Help yourself to the best leaves you'll ever taste. You're going to love the way these leaves make you feel."

Mac was puzzled. What was Roach talking about? But instead of questioning him, Mac began to nibble on the funny-looking green leaves. "These leaves taste different," Mac said. "Kind of bitter."

"Go ahead and eat some more," Roach urged. "You won't taste the bitterness in a few more bites."

Mac couldn't understand why he should eat leaves that didn't taste good. But he didn't want Roach to think he was a sissy. So he ate a few more of the bitter green leaves.

All of a sudden Mac started to feel strange. "I feel kind of dizzy," he gasped. "What's happening to me? Everything is so different. So, so interesting. Boy, am I hungry and thirsty!" Mac crawled to another twig and began eating more of the funny-looking green leaves. "You're right, Roach," he said a few minutes later. "I feel terrific!"

It wasn't long before Mac remembered he was supposed to meet Jeffery and Grace when the sun was high in the sky. "Roach, I've got to leave and meet my friends," Mac slurred.

"What's your hurry?" Roach asked. "We were just starting to have a good time. Come on and stay a while longer. Your friends will understand."

Suddenly Mac's old friends didn't seem as important as his new friend, so he stayed with Roach, and they ate some more of the funny-looking green leaves. Even Roach swayed with dizziness now. But he clung to a twig and told Mac stories that made both of them laugh. The two friends even talked about life in the meadow and how it would change once Mac became a butterfly.

"When I'm a butterfly," Mac bragged, "I'll be able to fly to the top of trees and see the whole meadow from the sky. Won't that be wonderful? I'll be able to fly through valleys, over mountains, and across lakes! It's even possible that I might cross the ocean on a big ship and go to England," Mac dreamed.

When the sun hung low in the sky, Mac again remembered his meeting with Jeffery and Grace. "Got to go, Roach. And this time, I mean I've got to go!"

ENGLAND

Mac was still feeling dizzy when he turned to crawl down the plant. As a result, he lost his balance and hurtled towards the ground. He tried to roll himself up into a ball as he and Jeffery did when they played Daredevil. But for some reason his body wouldn't curl up. THUD! Mac hit the ground hard.

"Ouch! That hurt!" he yelped.

Roach's laugh echoed across the field. "Are you all right, Big Guy?" he called. Then as Roach leaned over to see if Mac was really okay, he too lost his balance and went crashing to the ground. He landed in a crumpled heap next to Mac.

In the meantime Grace paced back and forth. She was worried because Mac was so late. "Do you think something awful has happened to him?" Grace asked Jeffery.

"I'm sure he's fine," Jeffery replied, even though he was starting to worry too. He decided to climb to the top of a milkweed stalk and watch for Mac.

When Mac finally staggered home, he knew he was in trouble. Grace was furious.

"Where have you been?" Grace scolded. "We've been so worried about you. Jeffery and I thought for sure a bird had eaten you or one of those jeeps that speed through the meadow had squashed you!"

Mac looked at Grace in a daze. "Mellow out," he slurred. "Get off my back! I'm all right! I had a little trouble playing Daredevil today. That's all!" Then Mac crawled under a milkweed leaf and went to sleep.

Very early the next morning Mac woke his two friends by telling them all about the new field of funny-looking green leaves he had discovered. He was excited as he told Grace and Jeffery how good the leaves made him feel. Mac didn't mention that the leaves made him dizzy and caused him to fall from the plant. No, Mac didn't tell Jeffery and Grace these bad things. He told them only what he thought were the fun parts.

"These leaves are the greatest! They'll make you feel terrific," Mac said. "You guys have got to come with me and try these leaves for yourselves. Will you come? Will you, Jeffery? Grace, you too?" Mac asked.

A few minutes later Mac led the way to the net-covered field. Jeffery and Grace followed.

When they reached the net, Jeffery felt very nervous. "It just doesn't make sense. Leaves that make you feel good. What kind of nonsense has Mac gotten us into now?" he wondered.

Then Jeffery saw the sign. "Mac!" he shouted. "Did you read this sign? It says, 'STAY OUT: DANGEROUS!' We shouldn't be here!"

Mac started to laugh, "There's nothing in there that will hurt us. The only thing under that net is a bunch of plants!"

"No, you're wrong!" Grace shouted at Mac. "Someone put this sign here because there is something in that field that can hurt you. It's bad for all of us! Now, let's go home and forget all about this place."

"Go home! I'm not going anywhere except through that net," Mac shouted. "I'm going to eat those funny-looking green leaves until I can't eat any more." With that, Mac wriggled through the net, leaving his two friends standing behind in shock.

"Mac's never spoken to us like that before," Grace whispered. "What's gotten into him?"

"I'm not sure, but we better find out," Jeffery answered. So Jeffery and Grace wriggled through the net too.

"Mac was right! There's nothing in this field but plants," Grace said after she and Jeffery were inside the net-covered field.

"But something bad must be here," Jeffery insisted.

As the two caterpillars followed the path of eaten leaves, Grace looked all around to see if she could find a clue as to what was going on. She looked high and low. Then quite by accident, she saw an envelope lying on the ground. The words "Marijuana Seeds" were printed on the front of it. Grace stopped dead in her tracks. Jeffery, who was following close behind her, bumped right into her tail.

"Look!" Grace whispered loudly as she pointed towards the envelope.

"Marijuana seeds," Jeffery read out loud. "Mac's been eating marijuana leaves! No wonder he's been acting so strangely. He's high on drugs!"

When Grace and Jeffery found Mac, he was acting weird. Mac was talking and laughing to himself about ridiculous things.

"Hey guys, I'm glad you came. Here, have some of my special leaves," Mac slurred as he pushed a marijuana leaf towards Grace.

"No!" Grace told him. "Don't you know what they are? Those are marijuana leaves! They're drugs! They're bad for you. Very bad!"

"You're crazy," Mac said. "How about you, Jeffery? You'll eat some of my leaves, won't you?"

"No, Mac. I don't want drugs either," Jeffery said firmly.

"Well, I do!" Mac shouted. "They make me feel good. They're not hurting me."

"Yes, they are," Grace pleaded with Mac. "Drugs will mess you up. Soon they will control your thinking, and who knows what else they will do to you. We must get out of here and STAY OUT!"

"Oh, go away," Mac demanded. "Leave me alone. I'm happy here."

Grace tried to reason with Mac again and again, but he wouldn't listen. Not knowing what else to do, Grace and Jeffery went home to the milkweed patch, leaving Mac in the marijuana field.

Later that day, Roach found Mac high on marijuana and wandering around in a daze. "Hey there, Big Guy," Roach called. "I guess you like those special leaves of ours! If you like the way marijuana makes you feel, I've got some other stuff you'll like even better. How would you like to try some cocaine?"

Mac looked puzzled. "What's cocaine?" he asked.

"Cocaine! Some of us call it coke," Roach said. "Cocaine will give you a real buzz. Come on, Big Guy, come with me, and let the Roach show you the way!"

Mac followed Roach to his home, which was in the center of a group of rocks. Once there, Roach disappeared for a minute or two. When he returned, he held a pocket flower in his claw. From the flower, Roach poured a small amount of white powder.

"This, my friend, is cocaine. Your ticket to another world!" Roach said as he let out an enormous laugh. As soon as Mac took the cocaine, he felt as if he'd been struck by a bolt of lightning. It was such an electric charge that his eyes bugged out of his head. Everything seemed to be going so fast. Mac crawled first in one direction and then in another. He climbed rocks and then trees. He rolled in the soft grass and in the cool mud. Then Mac listened to the birds sing. Mac sang with the birds and then he danced. Mac couldn't be still. He had to be moving.

The days passed. After Roach had Mac hooked on cocaine, he pushed him to try another form of cocaine called crack. As Mac took these drugs he changed. He didn't care about anyone or anything except his drugs. He forgot all about Grace and Jeffery. He didn't care if they were worried or even angry with him. Mac didn't eat either. In fact, he wasn't hungry at all. All Mac wanted was more cocaine.

There were other changes in Mac, too. Mac was moody most of the time. He lied and stole from Roach now, and his memory and judgment weren't as good as they once had been. And because he wasn't eating, Mac was losing weight.

One day while Mac and Roach were high on crack they decided it would be fun to climb a pile of rocks. As Mac struggled towards the top he came across a wasp nest and decided to get closer for a better look. He thought he was a safe distance away, but actually his nose was almost touching the nest.

One of the wasps watching Mac said to the other wasps, "Who does this fellow think he is? I'm going to let him have it!" The wasp lifted her stinger and aimed it straight for Mac.

"OUCH!" Mac cried as the stinger penetrated the end of his nose. Then another wasp swooped down on Mac and stung him on top of his head. "OUCH! OUCH!" Mac screamed. "Leave me alone!"

As Mac jumped back to escape he fell. First he hit the sharp rocks. Then he fell through the branches of a tree. Finally Mac landed in a patch of stickers.

"YEE-Ouch!" Mac screamed. He jumped out of the sticker patch and landed on the soft dirt path. Every stripe in his body ached, and he lay there very still.

"Oh, Mac. You're so clumsy," Roach sighed.

Once Mac was feeling a little better, the two friends went back to Roach's rocks. There Mac rested. He was in real pain. His nose and face were swollen from the wasp stings. He had sprained his tail and broken four of his front legs during his fall. Mac was a mess!

"Hey, Big Guy," Roach said. "I know what will make you feel better. Let's have some more cocaine!"

As the spring days grew warmer and the time drew nearer for the caterpillars to form their chrysalises and become butterflies, Jeffery and Grace began to search for Mac. First they went to the net-covered field where the sign marked "STAY OUT: DANGEROUS" still hung. They thought Mac would surely be there. So Jeffery and Grace called through the net, "Mac, Mac, where are you?"

Slowly Mac crawled from behind the rocks outside the net and answered, "Why, here I am."

Jeffery and Grace could hardly believe their eyes. How could this ragged, thin caterpillar in front of them be their "Big Guy."

"Mac, we've come to take you home," Grace said. "It's time to change into butterflies."

To their surprise, Mac smiled. "Okay, I'll come home with you. Becoming a butterfly sounds like fun!"

When the three caterpillars returned to the milkweed patch, they each hunted for a special place to hang their chrysalises. Grace was the first to attach herself to a leaf and hang upside down. "See you guys later, when I'm a beautiful butterfly," she squealed. Then Grace's body swelled until she was so fat her skin split open. After she wriggled out of her old skin, Grace hung very still until the new surface hardened to form her chrysalis. She was now ready to change into a monarch butterfly.

Jeffery was quick to follow Grace. While his body swelled, Jeffery called to Mac, "Good luck, Big Guy. When we're butterflies, I'll help you kick this drug habit of yours, and we'll all fly north together." And then Jeffery gave Mac a wink before his skin split open.

“Habit! What drug habit?” Mac asked as he suddenly found himself alone. “I don’t have a drug habit! I can give this stuff up anytime I want to!”

Mac waited and waited, wondering when he’d be ready to form his chrysalis. As he waited Mac broke out into a cold sweat and started to shake all over. He wanted more cocaine, and he wanted it badly.

Finally, early the next morning, Mac hung upside down from his leaf. Before long his chrysalis was hard.

Mac, Jeffery, and Grace were all tucked away in their chrysalises, changing into monarch butterflies.

Two weeks passed before one of the chrysalises split open. Out popped a beautiful orange-and-black monarch butterfly. The orange patterns on his wings were brilliant, his spots were as white as snow, and the dark veins were as black as black could be. He was very handsome.

As the new butterfly hung upside down, allowing his wings to dry, he marveled at the changes in his body. "Look at me! Look at me! I'm a butterfly!" Jeffery shouted for the whole meadow to hear.

A few minutes later a second chrysalis split open, and Grace pulled herself out of her sack.

"Well, hello there, slowpoke," Jeffery said. "Grace, you are beautiful. Will you fly north with me?" he asked.

"Of course I will," Grace giggled. "But we have to wait for Mac. He'll want to go with us."

Jeffery hesitated, "I'm not so sure. Mac may want to stay here with his drugs."

"Don't be silly! That was before we were butterflies and could fly!" Grace said. "Mac will be all through with that drug business. Just you wait and see. Everything will be as it was before, just the three of us."

Two days later, while Grace and Jeffery were flying above the milkweed patch, Mac's chrysalis split open and Mac came out. The first thing he saw were his two friends soaring high in the sky. He wanted to fly up and join them, but his wings would not flutter.

Mac looked at himself and then at Jeffery and Grace. He was different. His wings were all wrong. Only the bottom half of one wing had formed, while the other wing was too small and thin to support his weight. He tried, but Mac could not even flutter them. Mac's legs were so weak and crippled that he could barely hold on to his chrysalis. And his body hadn't changed into the slender black body of a monarch butterfly, but instead it was still the body of a shriveled caterpillar. Mac was deformed.

Mac was scared. He cried out to his friends for help. Jeffery and Grace hurried to meet Mac, but when they reached him, they couldn't believe their eyes.

Mac cried out, "What happened to me? Why didn't I change into a normal butterfly as you did? What went wrong?"

Grace and Jeffery helped Mac down from his chrysalis and placed him on the soft grass under the milkweed plant. "This can't be happening to our Big Guy!" Jeffery whispered.

But it had happened. Mac was deformed. "Why me? Why me?" Mac cried. "What did I do to deserve this?"

"Mac, it must have been the drugs you ate," Jeffery said. "They must have stopped your growth so you couldn't develop into a butterfly. I'm afraid you did this to yourself."

"I didn't know drugs could do this to me," Mac said. "They always made me feel so good before. Roach never told me they would keep me from growing right. He never told me this could happen! I just didn't know!" Mac cried.

Several days later the small meadow was filled with excitement. Thousands of monarch butterflies fluttered and flew about everywhere. Clouds of butterflies filled the sky while others rested on rocks and fed on the flowers in the meadow. They were all waiting to begin their flight further north.

When Jeffery and Grace saw the butterflies, they knew the time to leave Mac had come. The three friends would have to say good-bye. Mac would have to stay behind, alone.

"Mac, we love you," Grace and Jeffery cried. "Why didn't you say 'No' to Roach and those drugs? If you had, you would be flying away with us now. Mac, we will miss you."

Mac's eyes filled with tears as he watched Grace and Jeffery fly away to join the other monarch butterflies.

"How lucky they are," Mac sighed. "They will see valleys, fly over mountains and lakes, and perhaps they will even cross the ocean and visit England. They will see and do all the things I wanted to do."

Suddenly, thousands of monarch butterflies brightened the sky. Their northern migration had begun. Mac watched as the butterflies flew north out of his meadow. As Jeffery and Grace swooped low to dip their wings good-bye, Mac cried out, "Good-bye, my good friends, good-bye!"

Mac was all alone now. He started to shake badly as his body craved more cocaine. But he tried hard to fight his desire for drugs. Mac was scared. He wrapped his front legs around his upper body and hugged himself tightly. "Why did I use drugs?" he cried. "I had a choice. All I had to do was say 'NO'!"

THE END

Now that you have experienced Mac's story and learned about the pain that drugs can cause, we encourage you to read and discuss **Mac's Choice Workbook**. This workbook can help you be prepared for the day when **you** must make your own personal choice about drug use.

"None of your children were born winners or losers—but they were all born choosers."

Reggie Smith

About the Author

Debra L. Wert was born in Washington, D.C. and raised in Camp Springs, Maryland (a suburb of Washington, D.C.). She is one of seven children in a family that has grown, through marriages and births, to twenty-four. She attended the University of Maryland and received a Bachelor of Arts degree in Art Education. After several years in the field of education, Debra began writing and illustrating children's stories. This is her first published work. She now lives in the countryside of northern Virginia, where she paints and writes.